THE STORY OF DAVID & SARA PAULS:

From Alexandertal to Arnaud

CENTENNIAL EDITION:

Compiled in memory of the 100th Anniversary of their arrival in Canada, 1926-2026

Formatting and layout by Jadon Dick

Further editing provided by Earl Davey

Published by:

www.SchleitheimPress.com

Schleitheim Press is an imprint of

Okanagan Publishing Inc
1024 Lone Pine Court
Kelowna, BC V1P 1M7
www.okanaganpublishinghouse.ca

Printed in the United States of America

1st Edition, February 2022

10 9 8 7 6 5 4 3 2 1

ISBN: 978-1-990389-06-1

CONTENTS

Foreward:

100 Years of God's Faithfulness

This edition of the David and Sara Pauls' family story was undertaken to commemorate the centennial of their coming to Canada in 1926. God permitted them to escape the fate that befell so many of their friends, who did not get permission to come or chose to stay in the Ukraine after the communist revolution.

In spite of facing an unknown future, they decided to emigrate to a land that would permit them to live out their Anabaptist convictions and pass them on to their children. This also occurred at the time when Canada was looking for new immigrants. They were needed to farm the Prairies, in order to produce grain to send back east on the newly-built Canadian Pacific Railroad.

This retelling of David and Sara's story is also the impetus to launch a project of gratitude to God. Over the century since they came to Canada, God has led their descendants amazing ways. He has allowed us, their grandchildren, the opportunity to attend Bible schools and universities, which in turn provided vocational skills, opening doors to varied professions and the privilege of serving God in that way.

In compiling the list of addresses, it was humbling to see what a wide scope of influence many of David and Sara Pauls' descendants had. Some of them were recognized by their positions of employment, while others served faithfully at home, raising godly children, being active in the church, often in a music or helping capacity.

I regret not being able to provide additional information from some of the families, as many of them are already in Glory. Our oldest cousin, Sara Durksen, will be turning 100 on March 25, 2022.

- Elfrieda Dick on behalf of the cousins, March 2022

About:

Grace Children Ministries

At Schleitheim Press, one of our core Anabaptist principles is looking beyond our individual selves and towards the broader community. **Each book or resource we release is tied to a Christian charity or not-for-profit, and all net profit earned from *The Story of David & Sara Pauls* goes towards Grace Children Ministries (GCM).**

GCM is a non-profit organization helping orphans and vulnerable children, who are either on the streets or living in poor families. The ministry is based in Rwanda, Africa, and since then has helped over 500 orphans. GCM aims at changing children lives by providing them with education, household materials, medical care and food supplies.

Grace Children Ministries was formed in the aftermath of the Rwandan Genocide. This event devestated the region, and left behind a myriad of problems that didn't have easy solutions. These included poverty, over one millon deaths, millions more who survived the genocide but suffered severe trauma, and countless female rape victims who then gave birth to unwanted children, or were infected with HIV and/or other STDs.

In this environment, many people denied the existence of God. They would inquire, *"How would God allow this to happen if he existed?"*

When Pastor Semahoro Evariste and Fidele Ntagawa had a prayer time asking God what he could do, God gave him the verse Luke 18:27 *"What is impossible with the man, is possible with God,"* and a calling to help orphans, vulnerable children and single mothers that rejected by their families. They founded GCM on this vision in 2005, and today over 50 orphans and vulnerable children, plus 56 single mothers, are all being supported by the ministry. They have also founded Agasaro Nursery School to help the orphans and other children from poor families attain fundamental education.

To learn more about Grace Children Ministries

or to donate, go to *https://gcministry.org/*

PART ONE:

LIFE STORY OF DAVID & SARA PAULS

David Franz Pauls (born Apr. 23, 1871) and Sara Dückman, (born Nov 19,1877), were married in Dec. 18, 1896, and lived in Alexandertal, Molochna, Ukraine, South Russia. Together they raised a family of 12 children.

- ***Sarah (1897 – 1969)***
- ***Anna (1899 - 1983)***
- ***Martin (1900 - 1972)***
- ***Katherine "Katja" (1902 - 1998)***
- ***David (1903 -1990)***
- ***Liese (1905 – 1920)***
- ***John "Hans" (1907 - 1995)***
- ***Maria (1909 - 1988)***
- ***Helena "Lehna" (1911 - 2011)***
- ***Heinrich "Heinz" (1913-1928)***
- ***Greta (1915 - 1928)***
- ***Jacob (1919 - 2012)***

Pauls Family Reunion, 1944 (Listed as couples, L to R): *John & Mary Pauls, David & Lenchen Pauls, Martin & Gatha Pauls, Peter & Lena Braun, Jake Pauls, David & Sara Pauls, David & Sarah Durksen, John & Anna Thiessen, Paul & Katherine Wallman, Jacob & Mary Braun.*

EARLY HOME IN RUSSIA

Our grandparents[1] were hard-working, progressive farmers. When the Revolution broke out in Russia, 1917, shortly before their last child was born, Grandpa was considered to be a prosperous man, having built up a new farmstead in 1906 which included barn, house and storage shed as typical model of that day in the villages of the Molochna Colonies. Behind the farm lay the garden and an orchard that would have been a children's paradise with its variety of apple, apricot, plum, cherries and pear trees, not to mention all kinds of berries. The orchard ended at the banks of a tributary of the Uschanlee River which ran alongside the village. The seasonal flooding of this stream was the highlight of the year for the children, and then a member from each household would have to come help rebuild the bridge again so traffic could proceed to the fields which lay beyond. Besides the grain and alphalfa and barley that were grown, there were also big gardens of watermelon and beans, cabbages, and root vegetables.

Childhood Experiences

Since theirs was the last farm on the street, Grandfather's place was also close to the woods and a huge pasture and horse corral where the village colts were broken in every year. Uncle David recalls many hair-raising experiences in this regard. Since his brother Martin was less daring, Grandpa would lift David onto a bronco and say, "Son, hang on," He would hit the ground many times before the job was done and the gelding would be 'broken in'. The boys would also have great fun racing their horses

1 Due to the propensity for the names "David" and "Sara" in the Pauls clan, along with the book being written from the perspective of their grandchildren, the author has chosen to use the terms "Grandpa" and "Grandma" to distinguish these principal players.

and taking them to the river to wash them down. Grandpa was very fond of his 10-12 horses and took great pride in driving a well-groomed team. Aunt Katherine remembers that as a pre-schooler, curiosity led her to come watch the hired Russian maids milk the cows in the open 'loafing-barn' area, getting into the corral where the village live-stock was being kept and she was mauled by a steer.

Her brother David chose the straw sheep-shelter as the place where he was going to experiment with making a fire. Fortunately neighbors coming out of the woods saw the smoke coming out of the barn before serious damage was done. He remembers his mother kneeling down with him there after the excitement was all over, thanking God for his gracious protection. But then came the pay-off - a walloping with the stick.

Grandpa believed in the verse: "He who loves his son chastises him," but in spite of being very strict, he was a generous provider and his children recall him often buying fish and grapes when the peddler came down the street. When it came time to process the fruit for drying and storing in winter, Grandpa would help cut up the apples, and pick cherries and hops along the riverbank. Childhood was also a time for play and after their chores were done, such as sweeping the large yard, the older three sisters spent many hours of enjoyment with the Funk girls, their cousins who lived across the street.

School

It seemed there were always four children attending the village school of which Tante Lenchen's father, J.A. Toews was the teacher. Aunt Katja remembers it as a happy time as they set out with their lunch pails filled with brown bread, 'Grübenschmalz (fine cracklings) or sausage. Because she was such a capable pupil, she completed her schooling in five years, and since her parents didn't want to send her away to Maedchen Schule (a private Girl's school), she stayed home for two years and later went to High School with her brother David for three years. Because of her sturdy build, she had to work alongside her brothers doing chores and harvesting. Anna did the milking and Sara helped with the inside work.

Bread-making

Bread-making was a major undertaking. The night before, the huge baking troughs, half filled with flour, were carried down from the attic. Then a huge casserole of yeast was set to rise. In the morning the kneading began. What a job to keep a family of twelve children always supplied with bread. After, the huge white bread (Bulka) and four dark loaves were put on long trays and baked in the wall oven which was usually heated with straw or dried pressed manure bundles.

Harvest

Harvest-time was something you were happy to have behind you. The dust, heat and weariness all took their toll and Aunt Katherine recalls that guardian angels must have been doing double duty as the girls were expected to handle the 8 horses in front of the threshing machine amid the impatient shouts of men-folk, also overtired and impatient. The three girls often had to work behind the machine, separating the chaff from the wheat. Grandma had to keep everyone fed and even sometimes help to unload the bundles into the machine. Often their teacher, Johann Toews, would come help during threshing time. The grain was hauled home in three 'Leiter' wagons.

Now came the cleaning of the grain. All the grain had to be put through the 'Putzmühle ', a hand-operated winnowing mill where the final chaff was separated from the wheat. This was funneled into sacks which were lifted onto the men's backs and carried into the attic for storage. Grandpa would go barefoot, and in the evening enjoyed having one of his girls wash his feet.

Leisure

In the evenings the family would often sit on the veranda and make music. Both Grandparents had. lovely voices, soprano and tenor, and knew many songs for memory. They owned a pump-organ, two guitars and a balalaika which only Aunt Katja played. The latter was a Slavic variation of the guitar common among Russian and gypsy folk. How they enjoyed those evenings of song and often an old man would come and ask to have them play for him.

Sarah's Marriage

When Sara was to be married to David Durksen, the family spared no efforts to make the occasion a memorable one. Their love for one another seemed to have blossomed during the many times the choir went to sing at the windows of those who were sick or bereaved. Everyone was co-opted into the wedding preparations. The entire yard and garden paths were swept and strewn with yellow and white sand. The whole garden was raked and the stones bordering the flower beds were whitewashed. A huge bower over-laid with green branches greeted guests at the entrance gate. The wedding took place at the church in the centre of the village, but the reception program and was at home. The younger siblings (Geschwister) learned poems and songs for the occasion and looked up to their new brother-in-law with great respect. The young couple left to study in a Bible School in the Crimea. The family also had great admiration for their oldest brother Martin who was in Alexanderkron at the College, studying to be a teacher. He would come home on weekends, wearing a student uniform and often brought some colleagues along.

David & Sara Durksen (Listed L to R): *First Row - Sara (Pauls) Durksen, Clara, Agnes, Viola, Jakob, David D. Durksen, Mary. Second Row - Helen, Kae, David, John, Arthur, Sarah, Alfred.*

David & Sara Continued

After moving to Arnaud, MB, David worked on a farm and served as a lay minister in the local church. In 1948 they moved to St. Catherarine's, ON, joining the Braun clan there. They bought an orchard and together worked hard, the children in canning factories and picking fruit. David Durksen proved instrumental in establishing Eden Christian College, and all their children attended there. After retirement their children Sarah and Kae cared for Sara, who developed dementia. Eventually she moved to the Tabor nursing home, which David helped found, where she died at age 74. David would live until he reached age 92 and through everything was a faithful prayer warrior.

Spiritual Life

Spiritual values had a high priority in our grandparent's life in Russia. Their faith in Jesus Christ as Saviour and Lord of their life found practical expression in their daily activities. Their world revolved around the home and church. Grandpa was a 'Vorsanger' (cantor) in the church. Because there was no instrument in the church someone would have to start the song off at the right pitch. Unfortunately, because of his high tenor voice, he would often begin too high. He sang in the choir with his daughters and Martin for many years. His sanguine temperament drew him to people, and he enjoyed company immensely, offering to take guests home for Sunday dinner or for the night. Itinerant preachers often stayed at their house. The blessing of this hospitality had its effects on the children as well. As the whole family gathered in the front room for evening devotions, the minister would often ask them if they had already accepted Jesus as their personal Saviour, so they were aware at an early age of the importance of conversion. Aunt Mary recalls already having accepted the Lord at the age of 13 when she and three friends visited at the home of their cousin and youth leader, D.K. Durksen. One of the four village teachers was usually kept for room and board at their home, even though Grandma had her hands more than full with her growing family.

Grandpa Pauls was also very active in making house visitations, usually with another brother from the church. His team and carriage were also available when ministers needed transportation to another village. His gregarious nature and willingness to become involved in any work that needed doing, necessarily left Grandma at home with the raising of the children. Aunt Mary recalled that her older sister Anna was like a mother to them, and they usually took any problem to her because their mother was so busy with other duties. Because there was no Sunday School in the earlier days, Grandma would often stay home with the little ones. On Sunday morning and they would have their own service together, reading scriptures, singing many gospel songs and praying. Uncle David and Jake both recall the impact these prayers had on them, where Grandma poured out her heart before the Lord. They usually ended up weeping with her, and no doubt this accounts for the strong emotional element that is so prevalent in the Pauls clan.

Community Involvement

Grandpa was very active in community affairs as well, always carrying his load when there was work to be done. He strongly supported the movement to get a Fortbildungschule (High School) started in Alexandertal. He had the respect and love of all the villagers. He also had many friends the among Bulgarian and Russian people who lived in the surrounding villages and who felt free to come for visits frequently, so that Grandma got used to setting extra plates at the table. He also enjoyed auctioneering and was often called upon for that task, especially at the time of the emigration when many people sold their properties.

Martin's Marriage

As the children grew older, they left home one by one. Five years after the Durksens were married, Uncle Martin decided the time had come to be married to Agatha Suderman, his sweetheart from school-days. They had managed to carry on a discreet romance all the of his years of study and now that the Revolution years had brought studies to a stand-still even at the University in Halb-Stadt, they were finally of age to be married. Shod in shoes she had made herself, wearing Aunt Sara 's too-big wedding dress and with the groom attired in David Durksen's dark jacket, the couple took their vows and began their married life, living with one of the parents. It was the terribly difficult winter of 1921-22 in which many people died of starvation. The following summer their daughter Hilda was born and Uncle Martin got a teaching position which he held until they emigrated to Canada.

Martin & Agatha Pauls (Listed L to R)**:** *First Row - Ernest, Hilda, Waldemar, Elsa*
Second Row - Martin ,Ferdinand,Agatha (Suderman)

REVOLUTION

Grandpa's family faced great hardships as well, when roving bands of soldiers ravaged through the villages, plundering, looting, raping and killing. He was often in great physical danger, having to confront the threatening anarchists. The younger daughters recall coming upon him in the barn or by the woodshed where the kindling was split, crying to God for mercy and protection for his family. And God saw them through. The new Communist government requisitioned their horses to be for army use, so they could not work the land.

It was now that his generosity paid dividends. The Russian and Bulgarian friends he had made, often brought 5-10 lb. bags of flour or cheese made from sheep's milk. Then Grandma would cook a milk soup and no one had to hunger. But food was so scarce, they were forced to fry weed-greens (Käse-kraut) and catch sparrows to cook into a soup. Besides the havoc created by the political upheaval, it was also a year of drought, and with no reserves to draw upon. The people were desperate. Uncle David and his brother David Durksen one day butchered their pet dog Wollji and the meat was made into hamburgers. Corncobs were ground into flour to bake bread but many got sick from it because it was too hard to digest. But the family believed God to carry them through this difficult tine and He honored their faith.

Katja's Career & Marriage

Aunt Katja had made the decision to go to nursing school in Marija after completing High School, much to her father's sorrow. "It's just like burying you," he said at her departure. Later however, he changed his mind, and when she nursed both Grandma and him in his old age, he was ever grateful to her.

After her training was completed, she worked as a nurse in Muntau-Halbstadt, and later in Bethania, where the Mennonites had established an institute for the mentally ill and handicapped. Now she could come home only on holidays. She worked mostly on the 4th floor among the deaf-mute ward, where the most difficult patients were. Later she was put in charge. Because of her strong physique, she was able to handle them.

Here she also met Paul Wallman, who was the CEO, whom she later married. The first time she brought him home to meet the family, the younger sisters were very excited, having been told to be on their best behavior, as Paul came from a family of means, his father being co-owner of the Lepp-Wallman Factory, which had manufactured the first combine in Russia and won first prize at the Agricultural Exhibition in Moscow. Added to that was the fact that he didn't come from the Mennonite Brethren tradition and this would put her church membership in jeopardy. However, he never once let them feel that they were socially inferior, and with his droll humor soon won the hearts of the whole family.

Paul & Katherin Wallman (Listed L to R): *Herman, Katherine (Pauls), Paul*

Anna's Marriage

Two years earlier, John Thiessen, friend of the school teacher who had been staying with the family for a time, came to ask the hand of Anna in marriage. It was a far-reaching decision to make, but through prayer and consultation with her parents and the Durksens who were living with them, she consented. It was especially her brother-in-law, who gave her the verse from Isaiah 43:1-2, to help her make her decision, who also became her husband's closest friend. Her fiancé gave her a choice as to what she would like for a wedding gift: two expectant ewes or gold wedding bands. Seeing her dilemma in making the choice, he smilingly said he would try and get her both. He would twist binder twine into ropes and sell it, a commodity that fetched a good price, and so love found a way, even in that time of deprivation and financial need. They had a beautiful engagement service and wedding party and the Thiessen family was impressed with all the recitations, singing and music. No doubt the hard times had helped to focus thoughts on values other than materialistic. It must have been difficult for parents to let a daughter go, knowing how uncertain the times were. Aunt Mary remembers saying a poem specially composed for the occasion that bemoaned the siblings losing their big sister. They wondered if Aunt Katja should be asked to come home to help out, but ending by saying, "It will be aright because Mary at fourteen was quite proficient at mending clothes already."

Their daughter Liese died at the age of 15, after a lengthy illness, although none of the family make reference to it. No doubt it had a very sobering effect on the whole family. Death and danger were so prevalent at that time; heaven was a very present reality.

John & Anna Thiessen (Listed L to R): *First Row - Selma, John Sr, Henry, Irene, Anna (Pauls), Anne. Second Row - Eugene, Harry, Jake, John, David.*

David's Escape

David was at the age when young men were conscripted for military service, and because he was a conscientious objector and the political situation was vacillating, he was sent home for an indefinite period of time. At that time the Red & White Armies were warring through the villages, and any citizen could be conscripted to driving provision etc. He experienced several very close calls where the angel of the Lord rescued him from certain death. On one occasion he was forced to drive a load of soldiers back to their camp. They tied him up in a lonely stretch of enemy territory and made off with his team. After repeated struggling, David was able to free himself, and walk home, dragging the ropes behind him. Meantime, his parents were pleading with God for the miracle which brought him back unharmed.

EMIGRATION

Many of the Mennonites wanted to emigrate to Canada where there was new land opening up and where they would be free to live out their faith without fear of reprisals. They were no longer permitted to have their own teachers and teach their children. Even though the economic prospects under Stalin's five year plan seemed to offer some hope, their spiritual survival as a people was in great jeopardy.

Benjamin B. Janz, chairman of the Union of Citizens of Dutch Descent, (VBHH), had made repeated trips to the government in Kharkov. At risk of his life, he was finally granted permission to facilitate the exodus of over 20,000 Mennonites to emigrate to Canada. (Details of this memorable history can be read in his biography, *With Courage to Spare*, by John B. Toews.)

Meanwhile, David Toews of Rosthern, Saskatchewan, was the statesman in Canada who negotiated with the government of Mackenzie King and the Canadian Pacific Railroad to have these families settle on the prairies. Canada badly needed farmers to produce much wheat to be shipped to the East on the CPR, so that they would not have to return the empty rail cars that had brought the manufactured goods to the West. It was a task that required expert negotiation skills and perseverance. He and B.B.Janz had personally committed themselves to paying back the debt to the CPR which had been incurred when it had advanced the payment of travel fees for the immigrants. (*Many children still recall the family's hardship of saving the extra cash in the depression years, to pay back the "Reiseschuld."*) Both of these men later spent years and many tedious months of travel, away from their families, soliciting in the churches for the collection of the final last repayments. On his deathbed, Toews received the good news, "The debt is paid." and so their joint integrity was redeemed.

*(*At the 50th Anniversary celebration of the M.B. Church Coaldale, AB, B.B. Janz invited Col. Dennis of the CPR to be given a citation, and told him, "You saved our lives." This was an honor that deeply touched him, as he received it with tears in his eyes).*

In Aug. 1925, the David Durksen family left for Canada with a group of credit passengers. In November, Grandfather and his six unmarried children, (with the exception of David, who couldn't obtain his visa because of conscription), set out for Moscow, but was unable to get clearance because of Heinz' sick eyes (trachoma). Since John and Mary were both over 16, their passes were signed onto John and Anna Thiessen's list, while their parents with the four youngest children returned home to Alexandertal. This time of separating from the children was especially hard on Grandma. But now, there was no home to return to, everything having been sold. What a time of uncertainty.

They found temporary shelter with Grandmother's sister, the Jacob Durksens in Hirschau. It was the dead of winter. Then they stayed several months with the Jacob Pauls' in their home village, who had no children and weren't accustomed to the commotion of a big family. All six slept in one room, although there were other arrangements that could have been made. That was a very difficult time for Grandma, having to impose on a meticulous sister-in-law for an indefinite period of time.

So they ventured to Moscow a second time -- again unsuccessfully. It was May by the time they set out the third time, determined to stay in Moscow until they would get permission to leave. The house they stayed in was the same one C.F. Klassen stayed at and he did his best to get help for them.

One day Grandpa came back from a visit to the Doctor with Heinz, announcing jubilantly that they had permission to go! How they praised God! Now began the journey on the train and through the Red Gate into freedom. (The docudrama *And When They Shall Ask* depicts this vividly.)

But in Atlantic Park, England (a former army barracks, where other detained persons were housed,) their faith underwent another severe testing. *Heinz' eyes again didn't pass inspection.* He had to remain behind with other immigrants. Grandma's heart just about broke. How hard it was for the parents to have to leave their good-natured, 13-year old son behind, but Heinz had a strong faith and was able to join the family a year later.

Meantime, the Thiessens, who had taken on the responsibility of John and Mary, experienced a very turbulent journey over the Atlantic Ocean, often fearing for their lives. They arrived in Winkler, Manitoba, Jan.1,1926 and went to Hochfeld where the Durksens already lived, renting a very tiny house at the end of the village. (Aunt Mary can't imagine how they all fitted into it, but she has warm memories of being loved and cared for by the Thiessens). She got a job working for an English doctor in Winkler and took evening classes to learn English and sang in the Immigrant Choir. But everything was so strange and she was so homesick for her Geschwister and brother John. They had pity on her and let her stay with them in Hochfeld until they moved to Arnaud.

By spring, Martin and Agatha and girls had also arrived and so he and John and their brothers-in-law Thiessen and Durksen set off to look for land to purchase. They bought a section near Arnaud with only a granary on it. They rented a little house 1 1/2 miles away in which the families temporarily lived, while John and Mary made do in the granary, Mary cooking for the men and the hired carpenter as they constructed the two houses. These were situated only a calling distance apart, with an extended yard between them, designed in the style of homes in Russia. The living quarters on one end and barn on the other, with only a thin board wall separating the two sections. Invariably the bedding and clothes soon took on the barn odors.

It mast be acknowledged at this point that God made the owner of this land willing to sell to the Pauls clan without one dollar down payment. In addition to that, he was willing to forward them the necessary money to purchase the building materials, farm equipment and ten horses, plus two milk cows for each family. *What an unexpected blessing to experience such kindness in this new land of opportunity.*

This is the house-barn that was build on the original 400 acres Grandpa owned. The house (featured on the back cover) that was built in 1940, by John and his father, was red brick siding, the lumber hauled from Steinbach, with lots of volunteer help that was paid $5.00/day. *Who's the man on top?*

Our Grandparents, with Lehna, Gretha and Jake arrived that summer as well, and moved into one of the complexes with Martin Pauls, while Durksens and Thiessens lived in the other. It was a very difficult beginning but they were happy to be in Canada. Grandpa Pauls was still hale and hearty and worked the land together with his children, pulling his share of the load at every job. Because the crops were only poor, and the income sparse, it became necessary for two of the families to strike out on their own. Thiessens bought a farm a few miles to the south with a large stone house on it. and Martin, together with his brother David farmed a place to the west.

David's Wedding

David, who had miraculously received his pass to come over in Nov, '26, was engaged to Lenchen (Helena) Toews. She was unable to pass her medical examination because of trachoma, and remained in Atlantic Park, England until Aug. '29, when they were married in the Arnaud Community Hall, as it was a big celebration. They had written 250 letters to each other during their three year estrangement. These were later translated by their son-in-law, and provide a memorable journal of those years and God's sustaining grace.

At first they lived upstairs in Martin & Agatha's house, and later in the emptied granary on their yard for several years. David Pauls engaged in very labor intensive irrigation farming, and after moving to Alberta eventually also had a big diary operation in Coaldale as well.

David & Helena Pauls (Listed L to R)**:** *First Row - Helena (Toews), Ernie, David, Anne. Second Row - Victor, Helen, John, Elfrieda, Margaret.*

Death of Gretha & Heinz.

The year 1928 was one filled with testing and trials, as death claimed two of their children. Heinz had arrived from England in the fall of 1927, a happy redhead, soon beloved by all who knew him. Gretha had picked up rheumatic fever in the winter, no doubt from exposure while walking to school in the cold and deep snow. Since there was no doctor, home remedies were tried, but to no avail. Then she got dropsy as well, and had to sit up in an easy chair day and night, as the retained fluid in her body pressured the heart too much. Her body and legs were swollen, breaking open in sores that had to be compressed. Grandma and Aunt Mary took turns caring for her. A few days before her 15th birthday she became worse. The family was gathered around her, singing 'Heimatslieder' when she suggested the song, 'Es geht nach Haus, zum Vatherhaus, wer weis, vieleicht schon Morgen,' (We're going home, we're going home, perhaps tomorrow already), singing along in her bell-like soprano. Then her face became transfixed, as if she saw some thing. "How beautiful!" she exclaimed. "What do you see, Gretha?" her brother David asked. Then her head fell forward and she died in her parents arms. There was a holy silence as Grandpa prayed and tears flowed freely. But she was home - released from her suffering. Since the roads were nigh impossible, getting to the cemetery was a real problem, with spring thaw in March.

Shortly after this, Heinz became ill. He was looking forward to Mary and Jacob Braun engagement, where tea and refreshments were to be served to the choir and young people for the occasion. But he had to be taken back to bed before the evening was over. Dr. Klassen from Morris had been called to diagnose his illness. Heinz had already applied for baptism earlier, and one day, shortly before Mary's wedding date, June 27, as his father sat at his bedside, Heinz asked him, "Do you think I'll go to heaven even if I'm not baptised?" Grandpa reassured him and asked him whether he would be to ready to go, to which Heinz replied, "Let's not talk about dying." Soon Dr. Klassen drove onto the yard. Heinz groaned while he was being examined, and seconds later he was gone. As the doctor left he said, "Now I know it was kidney stones." The parents grieved deeply but they knew their children were with the Lord.

Arnaud Cemetary

Mary's Wedding

Because of the funeral of her brother, Mary's wedding was postponed to July 5th. As her beloved "Jasch," Jacob Braun, came to get her, ominous dark clouds appeared in the east. By the time the service was on, it was pouring, but the sun broke through for a few moments after they got up from their knees at the marriage altar, symbolizing happiness in spite of tears. Wedding guests had to be pulled to the highway with tractors. Many people simply took off their shoes and stockings and walked home barefoot in the mud. But the couple was confident in the knowledge that God had led them together and happily left for their little room in the Braun parents' home. God continued to let the sunshine through in spite of dark clouds that beset their pathway.

The couple was blessed with 7 children, and farmed in Arnaud until 1951 when they moved to St. Catharines, ON, due to losing the farm in the 1950 flood. (Although the farm house that Jacob built still stands and is inhabited to this day.) Upon moving to Ontario, Jacob became a crane operater. In 1960 the family moved to Kitchener ON, where Jacob passed away in 1966. Mary moved to Kitchener to be with her children who were working for Schneider's and also cared for grandchildren. Mary moved into Tabor Home until her passing in 1987.

Jacob & Mary Braun (Listed L to R): *First Row - Jacob, Raymond, Linda, Mary (Pauls).*
Second Row - Marlice, John, Tillie, David.

Arnaud

Arnaud became the spiritual centre for many immigrant Mennonites in the surrounding areas. Br. Abr. Nachtigal, Heinrich Toews, and son-in-law David Durksen, were the ministers. The church had a good choir and lots of young people. Here again Grandpa did a lot of visitation while Grandma stayed home and prayed for blessing on his ministry.

Paul & Katja Arrive

Late in June of 1930, Paul and Katja, the last of the Pauls clan to come to Canada, arrived from Russia . They had been through difficult times, fleeing to Moscow and Germany, where their darling year-old son Paul died of diphtheria. But let Paul tell the story in his own words.

> "David and John got us from the C.P.R. station in Winnipeg with a car. Katherine and I and our 12-year old nephew Konstantin (Kostja)[2] moved in with the parents on the farm. John, Helen (Lehna) and Jake were still single and at home too. The Depression of the '30's had just begun. People who came from Russia with nothing but their lives did not get rich quick. If Katherine had been able to, she would have gone right back where she came from. But I thought I had never had it so good in my life. All the people were friendly, there was plenty to eat, a place to sleep, with the assurance that nobody would come in the middle of the night and take me away.

2 The boy was in danger of being killed by the communists, as he was an heir of the Lepp-Wallman wealth and Paul was asked to take him along.

Though there was great unemployment in the country, there was always something to do on the farm in the summer. Sweet clover was being harvested. Have you ever stooked freshly cut sweet clover? Those sheaves weigh a ton each. But that was nothing compared to the sheaves that David and Martin's new 10-foot binder produced. Imagine very tall wheat, cut by a binder that made extra-large sheaves, all tied to-one another.

What delighted me most were the many children of the three families - Durksens, Thiessens and Martin Pauls. They ranged in age from infants to 13 years, and more were added as the years went by. The boys took great pride in helping in the fields during threshing tine. The threshing outfit, consisting of a separator and a slow, powerless ' Titan' tractor, moved from farm to farm, wherever the grain was ripe and ready to be harvested. Each of the four farms supplied a team with hayrack and driver. I have never before noticed the presence of so many guardian angels with children everywhere and in and out of everything. It never seemed to rain during harvest in those years. Many a morning, waking up with a stiff back, unbendable fingers and aching arms, I wished for nothing more than rain.

Another job was cutting the sweet clover sheaves into chaff. Earlier, these sheaves had been piled in great many miniature pyramids, called stooks. John Thiessen Sr., was the expert at doing this, as it was important that the rain would run off and not penetrate the pile.

On one occasion when everyone was ready with hayracks loaded and men getting cold in the nipper fall air, Martin Pauls could not get his John Deere started. He had parked it in the barn the night before, so it would start easier. There were no starters on tractors so everyone had to have a try at cranking the flywheel. Finally in desperation, (time was being wasted and you don't know what that means to a time-conscious, 'bosija' Pauls) Martin put a little dry straw under the tractor, and lit a match to it. I made myself scarce, not wanting to be present were tragedy to occur. In a few minutes I heard the familiar put, put of the tractor. What had happened? The night before Martin had turned off the fuel valve to prevent any gas from leaking onto the barn floor. All at once he remembered, turned it on, and the warm John Deere started 1ike a charm.

The boys all wanted to become farmers, and I tried to show them that there were other ways to make a living, like going to school and learning a profession. This I now sometimes regret, seeing how the few that stayed on the farm became very wealthy.

Not to be forgotten are the gathering of the 'Pauls Bunch' for birthdays and pig butcherings and whenever relatives came to visit from afar. Where all the food came from and where it disappeared to, is still a mystery to me. There were no store-bought short cuts. Everything was baked at home in an oven fired by damp poplar wood. This is when the saying originated, "Children, the Zwieback taste good too." Try and feed a bunch of kids buns when they had waited patiently or not so patiently for their turn at the cakes.

The transportation in those days was something else. The roads were very dusty, but in an unexpected rainstorm, the wheels from the famous Red River gumbo required the driver to stop frequently to clear the mud from under the wheels which had clogged beneath the fenders. In winter, after the snow made the use of sleighs possible, roads were created across people's fields. A grain-box, fitted with runners, was loaded to capacity with passengers, the children heavily bundled up in the terrible cold. On Sundays, 2-3 trips were made to church and back. More progressive farmers had built so-called cabooses onto the sleigh, sometimes with a stove in them. The dangers of these improvisations passes imagination.

In conclusion, I would like to say, that I always admired the unity of the sons and sons-in-law in the farming. This was evidenced when a father with his bunch worked under conditions that could easily have led to differences and even disputes. The Pauls clan is evidence of the truth, that *"It is pleasant when brethren dwell together in unity"* Psalm 133:1.

These are the end of Paul Wallman's comments, but I am sure tribute must be paid as well to the tolerance and accommodation of the wonderful in-laws that God brought into the family.

THE DEPRESSION YEARS

During the Great Depression in the 1930s, Uncle Paul attended school and moved to Gretna to obtain a Canadian teaching certificate, while Aunt Katherine did housework. She was also called into the villages as a mid-wife and a massager. In return for these services, she received eggs, butter or some money. She also came to help on the farm one summer. They especially remember brother John as being one who did much for them. The year that Paul attended Normal School in Winnipeg, Katherine had to have several major operations, but they also had the great joy of having a son, Paul Herman, born to them."

David with Lenchen, (along with baby Helen) was the only member of the clan to move away to Coaldale, AB. in the fall of 1931, to help operate herfather Toews' farm, Martin Pauls and he having farmed togther until then. (They would return every three years to visit and bask in the warmth of the extended family circle. If it is true that the Paulses work hard, it is also true that they love easily and intensely. When it came time to say good-bye, after the kisses and hugs were done, there were many tears of farewell.)

Aunt Helen (Lehna) remembers how as a teen, when she was taking the cows to graze on the pasture, she heard someone talk on the hedge close to the house. She found her father on his knees, talking to God. When Grandma would sometimes take the children's side in a matter, Grandpa would get very upset and say that she was just strengthening them in their laziness. Sometimes he could be very rough in his speech but his actions proved that he meant well. Grandma had a quieter nature, was very loving and also prayed much, although daughter Mary can recall receiving many an 'Ohrfeige' (smack) from her, as any growing girl would deserve from time to time.

The white building is the original house-barn with added sides for raising hogs, and the attic was used for poultry. Aerial view sent in by Werner & Margaret Pauls.

John & Mary Pauls (Listed L to R): Anne, John, Werner, Mary (Nachtigal)

John & Mary Marry

John married Mary Nachtigal, the minister's daughter in spring of '32, and her sweet, gentle nature was an asset to all. as they lived and farmed together with the parents as before. Hers was the gift of service, as she was not privileged to be in charge of her own household until Grandpa remarried.

Peter & Helen Marry

A year later, Aunt Helen fell in love with Peter Braun, her brother-in-law 's brother, and they were married Sept. '33. After the wedding the guests couldn't leave because the heavy rain washed out the dirt roads, so on his wedding night Peter would sleep with his brother-in-law, John Pauls! Eventually they moved into their own little house, where four children were born. In 1944 they moved to a farm in Niagara-on-the Lake, ON, and had another three children.

Peter & Lena were busy farming fruit. During this time Peter worked as an intern in the hospital by night and on the farm during the day, ensuring he could send his children to Eden Christian High School. Eventually they built a new red brick home, and had their final child in 1953. Every child would grow up knowing Jesus died for their sins, and at an early age they asked Him into their hearts.

Peter retired in 1973 after working a few more years at Linhaven Home. Four years later, they sold the farm and moved to a cozy bungalow, which was always open to hospitality. In 1987 they entered Tabor Manor where they lived for twenty years, each of them going to their reward, just months before reaching the age of 100. What a heritage - what a great and faithful God they were able to serve!

Peter & Helen Braun (Listed L to R)**:** *Peter, Helen (Pauls), Laura, Alvin,Teresa, Jake, Elsie, Peter, Eleanor, Mary.*

Trials & Tribulations

The purifying fires of tribulation came again to the Wallman family. While teaching in Plum Coulee, the doctor found Paul to have tuberculosis, and he had to enter a sanatorium. The dreams of a teaching profession lay shattered at his feet. Aunt Katherine and the baby were kindly taken in by the Thiessens. Then a dear old neighbor, Mr. Dearborn, worked out a $10 monthly support for her. After Uncle Paul was released several years later, the (Geschwister) siblings pooled resources and built a house and chicken barn for them in Arnaud. Aunt Katherine took in roomers; looked after babies, sold eggs and Uncle Paul found work at Isaac's store and paid back the loan.

Grandma had an ailment in her leg or hip and Uncle Jake remembers his mother only as a woman with a limp. She was seldom without pain, screaming in agony as she would lift her leg into bed. His heart would bleed at the sound and he would plead God to give her relief and a good night's sleep. In spite of this she managed to do her housework, but one can see what a blessing it was that Aunt Mary was there to help. Especially vivid in Uncle Jake 's mind were the long winter nights when John and sister Helen had gone off to choir practise and his mother would take all the old choir books with number notation and try to teach him the tenor line. She was an excellent reader of these Ziphern sheets. He would get cross when she expected him to sing it in the soprano range, but he was taught well enough that at the age of twelve, he could hold his own in the tenor section between George Sukkau and Isaac Goertz. How he admired his brother John for allowing him to sing in his choir at that early age.

When his mother's health was not good enough to attend church, it was Jake 's privilege to stay home with her and they would have a blessed tine of fellowship by themselves. When she was able to go, it was with pride that he would take her arm, the two of them walking across the church yard, past his teen-age friends, and in his heart exclaim, "This is my mother the worthy woman!"

New House

Grandfather was always very undertaking and optimistic about the outcome of a venture. In 1940 he decided the time had come to move out of the house-barn complex, and build a new, two-storey structure. This was duly accomplished with much difficulty and almost no money. It was a proud house, with brick, tar-paper siding, glassed-in front porch entrance, hardwood floors and French doors into the living room. Gradually Grandpa retired from the outside work, and let son John take over.

The new house on Grandpa's farm.

THE LATER YEARS

1944 Family Reunion

The David Pauls children can remember how exciting it was to come to visit their relatives - the 40+ cousins in Manitoba, to be invited to a different family's house for supper every night, and then to have all the other cousins come for the evening and play Prisoner's Base or volleyball together. The evening would always end off with a rousing singsong around the smudge fire, led by Uncle Jake, the most eligible bachelor-teacher in the area. I don't think we should underestimate the spiritual impact those times of togetherness had on us as younger cousins. Songs like "Leaning on the Everlasting Arms" and "When We All Get to Heaven" were new to us. Also memorable was the singing of the older cousin's male quartet. New songs with lyrics like "This world is not my home, I'm just a-passing through; My treasures are laid up, somewhere beyond the blue." Or "Gottes Volk kann nie Ermueden - Kaempfen muss es Tag fuer Tag." (God's people may not grow weary - engaged in the battle everyday.) The 1944 Reunion, at which the photograph of the family at the beginning of this book was taken, was particularly special. Shortly following this gathering the Lord called several family members home.

John's Passing

In 1945, John Thiessen died of a heart attack, leaving behind his grieving wife Anna and nine children. The burden of caring for the family and working the farm fell heavily on the shoulders of their oldest son Jake, who was then 21. Their second son John had been conscripted for alternate service as a conscientious objector during the war in Jake's stead, as he was needed for farming. Aunt Anna must have often been reminded of Isaiah 43:2, the verse that was given them at their engagement, "When you pass through the waters I will be with you." And God did sustain her.

Jake and Irma's Wedding

Jacob met Irma Schaefer, the love of his life, while boarding in the same home on his first teaching assignment. After a number of years of writing love-letters, they eventually married. Irma gave up a university scholarship to become Jake's wife. They lived close to the school in Arnaud where Jake taught.

After a brief attempt at farming, Jake taught at New Bothwell until they moved to St. Catharines where he worked as a bookkeeper. Jacob taught for many years after their move to Ontario and enjoyed his love of music throughout his life. Singing as a tenor soloist and in choirs as well as choral conducting gave him much pleasure. He also took great pride in his manicured gardens and well-maintained cars. After retiring from teaching he worked at the Tabor Manor retirement home in St. Catharines. Then, after receiving a set of golf clubs much to his surprise, he took up golfing and quickly learned to love the game. He also loved watching NHL hockey on TV and became the first person ever to have a satellite dish mounted outside his long-term care room.

Irma was a very energetic person who loved her family and friends. She was involved in founding a school for neuro-divergent children and became very respected for her work with them. In summers she taught special education courses for the Ministry of Education and also evening courses at Brock University. It was such a loss when Irma deteriorated suddenly and died from Creutzfeld-Jakobs disease at the age of seventy. Jake and Irma were able to celebrate their 50th anniversary just a few months before she passed away. Jacob died in 2012 at the age of 93, missing his 'dearly beloved' right until the end.

Jake & Irma Pauls (Listed L to R): *Ted, Jake, Ingrid, Irma (Schaeffer) and Peggy.*

Grandma's Passing

Grandma got more and more sickly. Dr. Klassen, Winnipeg, diagnosed it as liver cancer and Aunt Mary lovingly nursed her. Aunt Katherine came in the last days, and on Apr. 22, 1946, God called his faithful servant home. She was buried in the cemetery behind the church in Arnaud. She had so wished to be at the marriage of her youngest son Jacob, and was engaged to Irma Schaeffer, the daughter of the long -time principal of the Gretna Collegiate Institute.

Grandpa Remarries

Grandpa Pauls married Helen Riediger Loewen in August. of that same year. This second mother had a sunny disposition and Uncle John and Aunt Mary remember many fun times together in the three months they lived with them. Then they bought a little house in Arnaud, very close to the Wallmans. Unfortunately this marriage lasted only a short time as she died of a heart attack in Nov. 1948 and was buried beside his first wife.

Moving Away from Arnaud

In 1948 a mass migration to Ontario took place; Durksens, Thiessens, and Brauns all felt that opportunities for work and education for their growing teen-age families were more abundant here. Many of the boys found work at the General Motors plant, some worked in orchards and factories.

After Grandpa's second wife's death, he was very lonesome and in the spring of '49, went to Ontario to visit his children. Here he met another widow, Paulina Rempel, whom he married shortly after. They lived in Arnaud for two years after which they sold their house and joined the other children in St. Catherines in 1951. During this time Uncle Paul tried teaching once more, but it didn't work out and he suffered a nervous break-down, so they also moved East, Uncle Paul finding employment in a zipper factory and Aunt Katherine as a registered nurse.

Martin's family, after farming for 25 years, moved into Winnipeg where he trained as an orderly in a hospital and, after his retirement, worked at the Institute for the Blind. It was work he enjoyed, finding great gratification in being able to help people.

Uncle David and Aunt Lenchen, having sold their mixed farming/dairy operation in Coaldale, Alberta, semi-retired to Winnipeg. None of their sons wanted to become farmers, and the irrigation and diary needed hired help, so they went to be near their older children. They farmed some land near Lorette, MB, while their three younger children attended University and MBBC in Winnipeg. After ten years, they followed three of their older children who had moved to Clearbrook and retired there. During that time, they were always very engaged with their church, hosting and keeping in touch with all their relatives.

Final Days

Grandpa Pauls soon made many friends in his new home in Ontario. Anyone confessing Jesus as his Saviour from sin was his brother in the Lord. He distributed tracts and witnessed to people. On January 3rd, 1953, he was confined to his bed from what was believed to be a light stroke, but it turned out to be a three-month siege of terminal prostate cancer.

Sarah Durksen, his granddaughter, nursing in the hospital, was assigned to his ward. She was a bit apprehensive, knowing Grandpa to be quite outspoken and brusque at times but he turned out to be and excellent patient. The men in the wing called him the 'General.' He refused to wear a hospital gown and so Grandma would bring him a clean white shirt to wear every day. This distinction no doubt helped to him earn the extra respect. Sarah said even in his coffin later he looked like a general.

His daughter Katherine nursed him at the end, and he was grateful for any service done for him. His three sons from Manitoba, Martin, John and Jake, were privileged to see him yet the day before he passed into glory, on Good Friday, April 3rd 1953. Our Grandfather had lived a full life. In all his varied experiences, he was an example to us in his steadfast faith in God and his word. We want to follow his example and be able to say with the Apostle Paul. "*I have fought the good fight, I have finished my course, I have kept the faith. Henceforth there is laid up for me a crown of righteousness which the Lord, the righteous Judge, shall give me on that day, and not to me only, but to all who love his appearing*" 2 Timothy 3:7-8.

Editor's Note: This compiled history of our grandparents was undertaken in conjunction with our Pauls Reunion, at Otterburn, MB, using materials sent to me by our aunts and uncles. I am especially indebted to Uncle John Pauls, who sent a very comprehensive report, as well as the Wallmans and Aunt Mary and Aunt Helen Braun. I trust we will all take time to read it and thereby gain a better understanding of the past and the enviable heritage that comes with it. Although far from complete, we would like it to stand as a tribute to our clan founders. Now each of the cousins have to write the rest of the story "of their own family's pilgrimage" and thereby pass the baton. - *On behalf of the grandchildren, Elfrieda E. Dick. June 24, 1978.*

We honour Sarah Durksen, our Centennial Cousin. She is the last surving member of the Pauls clan who came from Russia in 1926. She went to nursing school from 1950-1951, and was a Registered Nurse Assistant. We would like to remember her sacrificial service to her aging parents.

40+ Cousins in the '40's: (Listed L to R): ***First Row*** - Margaret Pauls, Verner Pauls, Jake Braun, Jake Durksen, Herman Wallman, Linda Braun (baby), Ferdinand Pauls, Jon Braun, Victor Pauls, Alvin Braun, Henry Thiessen. **Second Row** - Laura Braun, Clara Durksen, Elfrieda Pauls, Irene Thiessen, Mary Durksen, Theresa Braun, Viola Durksen. **Third Row** - Sally Thiessen, Helen Durksen, Kae Durksen, Tillie Braun, Anne Thiessen, Helen Pauls, Aggie Durksen, Anne Pauls, Dave Braun, John Pauls. **Fourth Row** - Else Pauls, John Durksen, Hilda Pauls, Jake Thiessen, Sarah Durksen, Art Durksen, Harry Thiessen, David Thiessen. **Fifth Row** - David Durksen (Inserted), Wally Pauls, Eugene Thiessen, Alfred Durksen, Ernest Pauls, John Thiessen (Inserted).

PART TWO:

THE TRIP TO CANADA 1926

Grandma's story in her own words - translated from German by her son Jake Pauls

In 1926, when many emigrated from the Ukraine, we also thought seriously of leaving. We often asked God for clarification. We did not have the means to leave. We asked God to show us a way to leave. Shortly after my brother, Henry Duckman wrote us that the money that he had in the Ukraine could be used for our departure. So we took this as being from the Lord. We would be able to pay him back when we arrived in America.

We began to work toward getting our papers (Passes) - about March just before the seeding time. We needed to go to Halbstadt and then to Berdjansk. I have forgotten how many times we made the trip. I think six times to Berdjansk and four times to Halbstadt. Then they sent the papers to Melitopol. We went there until they gave us the papers. Martin always went because he was best able to represent our cause as all the papers were in Russian. In addition, changes needed to be made every time the papers were recopied.

The roads were bad, but this did not prevent us from making the many trips, So the summer came to an end.

We did not want to sell the farm until we saw the Passes becoming available. We had several buyers for the farm but we continued to work as if we would not leave. We brought the crop in for winter. We cooked syrup from watermelons and put canned jars in the cellar. So all that was needed for the winter was done.

Then Katja came home from Bethanian where she was working in the mental institute. She wanted to get married to Paul Wallmann. Meanwhile David and Sara left for America right after her engagement. This was tough for us but the Lord helped. Then suddenly Heinrichs and Peter Pauls came and said that they wanted to try to leave before Christmas. They wanted us to leave with them as well. We worked hard to try to get our Passes.

We prepared for the wedding. Celebrated the wedding. They were prepared to stay while the rest of us emigrated. When it was feasible, Paul and Katja would follow. Two weeks after the wedding - the 10th of November - we had an auction sale. On the 17th of November we left Alexanderthal for the first time. We stayed the night with Jacob Pauls. On Sunday morning we had our farewell in the church. Many came to say good-bye. It rained hard all day as well as on our way to the train station. We went to Naljowka.

We arrived in the evening with five wagons. After we had unloaded them, we said goodbye to those who had brought us to the station. David had to stay as well as he was in the military service but on leve for an indetermined amount of time. He then bid usfarewell. Katja then went with us to Alexandrowsk. Got off from the wagon and drove to Bethanian to her Paul. That was not easy for all of us. We then drove to Jekateraslam. Martin and Agatha accompanied us to Moscow. In Jakaterasham we had to change trains. Arrived in the morning. Continued in the afternoon.

We arrived in Moscow Wednesday, in the morning of Nov.19 Three days since we left home. This was my birthday.

We waited all day in the waiting room. Many interesting things to see. At last in the evening we were assigned a place to stay. We needed to pay 20 rubles to bring our luggage to quarters. When we arrived we had to wait outside for some time. It was cold and was snowing, and the children were crying. Their feet were frozen and the same for the old people. Thiessens had come a day before. And they had their quarters. Then Hans Thiessen said to come to their place.

At this time Dad and Martin came and brought us to our room. It was one small room for 15 people. We stayed there 14 days. Martin and Agatha left for home on Friday. We stayed until Saturday. I need to go back a step. Thursday after our arrival we needed to go to see the Doctor.

It was as if we were going before a court of law. The whole family was called in order, first Father, then I and the rest in order until Jake. Heinz was called last. We were all good except Heinz could not go. This was as if a dagger through the heart. Father went to talk to the doctor and suggested that Heinz could go back to Alexanderthal, get medical care for his eyes and then come with David. The Doctor did not permit this. He said Heinz was too young at 13 and we should all go back to our village.

As Thiessens had passed their tests, John and Mary asked to go with the Thiessens. That was a heavy for us but we decided to repack their clothes and beds. On Friday the 21st of November in the evening they drove with Father and Uncle Thiessen in a car to the train station. That was a heavy night after Father came back. It took us a long time to go to sleep. Martin and Agatha had already gone home on Friday. The Thiessens and we went on Saturday. They could not leave as Greta had a growth and she was small in stature. The doctor would not pass her. We went to the train station Sat. and spent 10 hours on our way back to our home.

We cannot describe how heavy the burden was that we felt. We drove to Federowka and arrived at 3:00 p.m. and at 10:00 p.m. boarded the train to Stulnova. We arrived at 4:00 a.m. and hired a wagon from a small man Mr. Stobbe from Waldheim.. He drove us to my sister Durksen. We had breakfast and Gerhard drove us to Alexanderthal, our former village - yes our former home. We could not describe our feeling. We went to Father's brother Jacob Pauls. (David was staying there until he could emigrate.) As we came into the house we were greeted in a friendly way. The next day Father took Heinz to Alexanderwohl to see Dr. Dick. They stayed there until Christmas. (Flashback - Henry Pauls (Grossweide) had to return as well because of his eyes. His son Peter had come with his father as he was old and could not travel alone. They stayed with his sister, Peter Funk's, who kindly took Father and Heinz to the doctor. When they all came home for Christmas their eyes were all supposed to be healed.)

We decided to go to Moscow a second time, hoping that this time Heinz would pass the examination. We waited for Martin to receive his Pass. When he received it, we made preparations to leave- but with a heavy heart. Would Heinz be able to pass his medical?. On the 18th of January, a Sunday we and our four children, and Martin Pauls, drove to Stilkowka. We arrived in the evening with our sled. We said good bye a second time to our son David who went back to Alexanderthal and we waited for the train. At 10:00 p.m. we got on the train for Kharkov. Arrived Monday at 8:00 a.m. and at 11:00 a.m. we took another train. We arrived in Moscow on Wednesday at 7:00 a.m. We stayed in the waiting room for the day and then drove to our quarters to stay with Froeses - a German man and his Russian wife-very nice people.

Thursday morning we all went to Buskaya to see the doctor for an eye examination. It was impossible to describe how we were feeling. Father did not taste his food. He was numb. Heinz looked so sad that our heart was almost broken. It was as if we had done something bad and were now going before the court. Suddenly the doctor calls Martin and Agatha. They came out and had passed their exam. They were happy. Then the rest of us went through. When Heinz came forward the doctor shook his head and said *Heinz could not continue his journey.*

Father spoke again with the doctor who suggested that we stay in Moscow and wait for the eyes to heal. This was too expensive for us. The food was almost gone, the quarters needed to be paid for and each day we would need to drive to the doctor. Father thought it would be better to go back home. We wanted to leave Heinz here but he did not want to as all was strange and unknown for him. We said good bye to Martin and Agatha. They went on to America and we with Thiessens went back to Alexanderthal for the second time. That was Thursday. Friday Martin and Peter Pauls took us to the railway station. We waited for our train and left at 10:00 p.m.

At 2:00 p.m. we arrived in Fedrofka. That evening at 10:00 we left for Stulnov. When we arrived at 4:00 a.m., and there was a heavy snow storm and we were afraid to continue our journey. There was also no transportation waiting and it was cold in the waiting room. Suddenly transportation arrived. It was the little Stobbe from Waldheim that had driven us the first time we returned from Moscow. He said "Lets go... I know the way" We were very afraid. We had no footwear, no heavy blankets. The wind was very strong and it was cold. We got into the sled. The storm was very strong. Suddenly Stobbe said to Father he should take the reins. He would look for the road. We stood still. The children started to freeze. The horses had strayed from the tracks. Suddenly Stobbe said to come over. He had found the tracks. We cried to the Lord and the children could not be quieted because they were frozen. God heard us and we came at 6:00 a.m. to Hierschauer. All were sleeping. We woke them and we were allowed into a home. We warmed up and drank hot prips. When we had eaten dinner Gerhard drove us to Alexanderthal. We went to Father's brother Jacob Pauls again. When we stopped in front of the house, David, Trinke and Jacob Pauls came out of the house. Naturally they wondered why we had returned again but received us graciously.

So we stayed with Jacob Pauls from the 26th of January. On the 28th Father went with Heinz to Alexanderkrone to the doctor. Butner and I went to my sister's birthday. When Father came home with Heinz you should have seen the boy. His eyes were swollen shut - he had scratched them. Father explained how he had cried. Blood had run down his cheeks. They brought a bottle of Primotshka with them. They went morning and night to Martin Durksens to look after the eyes. Then twice a week to Alexanderkrone. The boy had to endure a lot. And yet he was always happy. When he thought that we had to stay behind because of him it made him sad.

During this time we have prayed a lot. Others with us. We experienced from all sides how many have helped us. We also experienced hours of blessing. We were depressed. Satan did not spare us. Again, and again - what will the people say? Just the opposite - we experienced only love and understanding.

We celebrated Easter. We had the joy that Paul and Katja came for Easter. We were very happy. Time went on to April. Then we slowly started to get ready and left on April 14 (3 ½ months later). That was Monday morning. Aron Pauls and Jacob Berg drove us with Peter Reimer's vehicle to Melitopol. Our David came with us part of the way. It was a nice day with hot weather. The first time we left it was raining. The second time snow, and now the third time, dry roads and nice weather. From Steinfeld, Abram Martens came with us. We went to a reception place where we fed the horses. Then we were taken to the train station where the train came at 10:00 p.m. David and Aron Pauls helped us get all our baggage on the train. We said goodbye to

David for the third time and then the train came and we were gone on our way to Moscow, not having to change trains. We arrived at 7:00 a.m, hired transportation and drove to our old quarters at the Froeses.

The next day we went to the Pykona to see the doctor. Martens had come with us and they passed the medical. We all except for Heinz had passed previously. The doctor said one eye of Heinz was good. The other had a spot that still needed to heal. He could not let him go. He said we should wait in Moscow for three weeks. That was too long for us but there was nothing we could do. Father went with Heinz to the specialist. He did what he could. Heinz travelled alone every day at noon with the tram It cost 13 rubles each way.

We stayed until the 19th of May. That date was important as our passes expired and we would have to have them renewed so Father wanted to have them renewed now and went to see the authorities every day. They said they felt badly for Father every time they saw him. They promised to help him when Heinz was healed. On the 15th of May Father took Heinz to the doctor while I and the children prayed. When the doctor saw Heinz he said to Father that there was one thing lacking. That really made Father depressed and he begged the doctor to let them travel to America. ***All at once the doctor turned to the table and wrote something.*** (A total miracle.) Then the papers were made ready. Heinz came to the quarters, and Father followed with the papers. When he came we had everything ready to leave. Father rented transportation, settled our account at the quarters and at 6:00 p.m. we left our lodging, and at 10:00 p.m. we were already aboard the train.

What did we all see in Moscow? So many green trees, flowers and green grass. It is nice in Spring. The birds sang, nature was nice very different than in winter, but even then it was nice when evergreen trees stood in the snow. We started our journey on

Saturday and arrived Sunday at 5:00 p.m. at the Red Gate. ***We slowly travelled through the Red Gate*** and found that people on the other side spoke a different language and were dressed differently. They were very friendly. We were in a different world. We were interested in everything. So we continued on to Riga where we arrived Thursday 9:00 a.m. The vehicles were standing ready to take us to our quarters. Upon our arrival we were given breakfast and then taken into the Banja. Our clothes were also disinfected-few needed to be discarded. We had dinner and then went to the barracks where we stayed one night.

Then we were brought to see the doctor where we had our physical exams. Those were heavy hours for us but God helped. As the doctor saw Heinz he thought he was sick because he looked swollen. He pressed his finger into his arm and asked if he had headaches, Heinz said he had never had headaches. Then it was my turn. It went OK. Then he was finished with us.

We went to eat dinner. When we were at the table an agent called Father and Heinz. Father arranged the issues with Heinz for 15 rubles and we were free to go. On Monday evening we took a car to the station . We waited in a large waiting room. We then had to climb many steps before we boarded the ship. At 11:00 p.m. we started our journey. Came on the 21st of May to Liebau. There we waited two hours at the water's edge until we were able to board our ship. When we had all boarded we were invited to dinner.

The ship left at 4:00 p.m, arriving in Danzig at next morning. Saturday and Sunday we were very seasick. The North Sea had many storms. But it was quiet on the Thames river. We had three evening services. A brother Franson from Dakota spoke. He and his wife had been to Germany. While on the Thames River in bright sunshine there was a concert with violin accompaniment. We arrived in London at, the afternoon of May 24th. We had to stay on the boat until the ship was allowed to dock. Then we still needed to stay overnight. We saw wonderful things – amazed at what man can think of. We went under a bridge. When we had passed, the bridge shut again and cars whizzed over, up to 14 at a time. We disembarked on the 25th, walked through a large gate and saw cars ready to take us two hours to our quarters. This was the 29th of May.

The next day we went to see the Doctor. The women were all combed for lice, I had it done twice. All eyes were good except Heinz. We were emotionally affected as Heinz was supposed to stay here. How we cried to God for strength and Grace for Heinz. In Moscow they said he could go to England and stay there but when it came now to stay, it affected him deeply. These were heavy days for us. Often we went alone to green pastures and prayed. When it was time to leave, we went with Heinz to a room in the Barracks and prayed. ***I will never forget that time.*** We took our luggage, Heinz helped carry, and stood in a room close to where we had our meals until they called us. We boarded cars that took us to our ship. Heinz stood by the door in a corner and cried. ***I will never forget that hour.***

We arrived at the wharf and passed through three stations. When all had boarded Father had to wait. They would not let me and Jake board until Father came. What a suspense. Suddenly he was there and we were able to embark. When all had boarded, the ship departed at 9:00 a.m. At 12:00 we arrived in France. Our ship was called *Empress of France*. It was a large ship. We Mennonites were 87 people. There were up to 1000 people altogether. We departed Saturday . The first three days we were very sea sick. The last days were very nice with lots of sunshine.

We arrived Saturday morning-exactly a week later in Quebec We disembarked, were looked at by emigration and taken to see the Doctor. In the afternoon we boarded a train and started our journey to our new home. What had we seen in Quebec! Land with stones and Felsen (rock formations). Also trains that travelled a lot faster than in Russia. We arrived in Winnipeg on Monday, the 7th of June at 1:00 p.m. We waited until 5:00 p.m. and boarded another train to take us to our home - Arnaud, MB. We were the only German speakers on the train. Father sat with an English man and showed him our tickets. The man showed him with fingers how many stops there were until Arnaud.

When we got off there was nobody there to greet us. We stood alone as strangers. Father went to look for Harders. (In Winnipeg they said that a Harder lived in Arnaud.) A man approached Father. His name was John Friesen from Lichtfelde. He said there was a Henry Duckmann from Pordenau. "Well, that is Mother's brother," Father said, "Lets go there." And really it was him. When we got to his place he was cutting weeds. Father shouted in low German "But really brother-in-law!" What a joy. They were living with Harders. Both women came to greet them. Who would have thought this? We needed to meet our relatives first. My brother looked so strange. He was wearing overalls that looked comical to me. Then we went to Duckmanns and had something to eat. Harder had phoned our children. They had just been to the train station. I felt like I was suspended between heaven and earth. Soon Hans Thiessen and Mary came with a car. They had asked their neighbor Nichols if they would get us from the station.

Editor's Note: *There is no record of the reunion although it must have been tempered by her sadness at leaving Heinz behind. We don't know to whom he was entrusted to as a guardian in England. He did join them a year later, but then died at 15. The legacy of God's faithfulness that we have inherited should not be taken lightly. I pray that we may all be able to guard what has been entrusted to us.*

PART THREE:

THE TIME THAT WAS

A Short-Story Reflection on the Trip to the Pauls Reunions in Arnaud

The letter in my hand could hardly be torn open quickly enough. Whatever would my oldest cousin in the Pauls clan be writing to me about? A reunion! After all these years and at the site of our many get-togethers.

Memories flooded my mind and soon I was again a fat girl of ten, making the tri-annual pilgrimage to visit the forty-plus cousins in Arnaud, Manitoba. Why was it that those trips were such a highlight in my childhood, which seemed shrouded in endless days of grey routine? At home I was simply a very ordinary, overweight, middle child in a family of six, whereas, when we visited our cousins, who gathered every night at the home of one of the well-endowed aunts' houses for games and singing, I took on the aura of some exotic princess, feted and fawned over by doting, teen-age cousins who were SO charming and handsome. And nobody would tease me about them being my boy-friends because, after all, they were my cousins.

It would all begin very unexpectedly. My father would come in for supper one night and announce,

"If it doesn't rain, and we can finish the haying and cultivate the beets, we can leave day after tomorrow." A cry of jubilation greeted this statement, followed by the clamor,

"How long can we stay? Can't we stay two weeks?"

"No, if we're lucky, it will be ten days because I'm expecting several heifers to freshen and I don't trust the hired man with them."

"Oh please, please."

"Well, we'll phone from Manitoba and see how the weather has been, and if the grain isn't ready for cutting, maybe we can stay a few days longer."

Our appreciation often overflowed in impulsive hugs and kisses, even though my normally non-demonstrative father acted as if this affected him not a bit.

Mother would go into a frenzy of preparation. Clothes had to be washed and ironed, fresh baking needed to be done to take along and the peas and beans in the garden that needed to be picked and canned, in view of our long absence, demanded attention.

The journey began in true farmer fashion at 4:30 a.m. My father was a firm believer in getting an early start, before the heat of the day was upon us, and of course one never knew what might befall one on a long trip. Crossing the prairies still had its hazards. The Trans-Canada highway of 1944 was newly gravelled, but if it rained you might still get stuck in places. As for now, we were keeping our fingers crossed that the car wouldn't overheat, because then Dad would have to scout about for a barrow-pit with some water in it, to fill up the radiator again. There were some long, barren stretches of uninhabited prairie to traverse, before we would reach our destination. Meantime, the four of us rearranged ourselves at the back of the car on our high seat of quilts (to help supply the bedding for our family at Grandma's house) and snuggled into our pillows, trying to catch up on the sleep we had lost with our early rising, our Plymouth purring along at the top speed of 45 miles per hour. Perhaps we would awaken to see the sun rise over the flat horizon and the morning mist lift slowly from the endless stretches of aromatic sage brush.

A lone coyote loped across the fields in the distance.

Reaching Medicine Hat was a small mile-stone. Mother would begin passing out sandwiches for our breakfast and Father would ask for one more cup of coffee from the big quart jar which was still hot because of the newspaper wrapping around it. After filling up with gas, and stretching our legs, we were off again, eagerly looking forward to passing the border into Saskatchewan, the dust from the road sifting in through the doors and windows.

By noon we had passed a time zone, set Father's watch back, and found a coolish spot beside some bushes in a ravine to eat our lunch. There wasn't a tree in sight, and the sun was climbing higher and higher. It was going to be a hot day.

"I told you we would be glad we got an early start," Father, would remind us. The canned hamburger on buttered brown bread was delicious. I watched Father carefully layer his with home-made, ochre mustard.

My oldest sister Helen was in charge of the map, calling out the name of the next town, while the rest of us, well fed, and bored with looking at the July landscape, with the assorted pigweed, sunflowers and sweet clover growing along the roadside, began snoozing again. My mother, with my baby brother Ernie on her lap and little sister Margaret on the seat between them in the front, were also asleep and soon her head would bob forward as she dozed off, but she resisted our entreaties to take a pillow, and lean against the window. "I'm just fine," she tried to make us believe. The after-shock of finally being on our way was telling on her. We were rudely jolted awake with the car stopping suddenly.

"What's the matter?" everyone asked at once.

"I think we have a flat tire," was Father's verdict.

Scrambling out, we found he was right and so began the unpacking ceremony to get at the spare tire in the trunk. This was a good time for a sip of cold, sweetened tea and a cookie.

Now we were on the look-out for a garage where we could get the flat tire repaired.

"Maple Creek is coming up in seven miles,"Helen announced.

We were permitted the luxury of exploring the town while my father and older brother John, already a teenager, checked on the attendant to make sure he did a decent job of patching the tube.

"How far is it yet?" came the worn-out question from younger brother, Victor.

"We should be in Moose-Jaw by night." Father predicted. Mother passed out Poresky (pie by the yard), a pastry proven to be a good traveller. To break up the monotony, it was decided to practise the song we were going to sing for Grandma and Grandpa. Our parents' voices blended so well together, Mom's high soprano and Dad's lovely tenor, the rest of us singing whatever.

The hotel was three stories high with a rickety fire escape. The district around it reminded one of railroads and dusty coal cars. We took the elevator up and entered a dingy, carpeted hallway. So many mysterious doors and big numbers! After dragging everything into the room, we could decide who slept where. On the wash stand was a rose-flowered porcelain pitcher and basin, and there was even a rug on the floor. Mother had opened the food box and pealed the boiled eggs for our supper which we ate with the rest of the whole wheat bread. There was also a bathroom for our use, and now we could retire like royalty, with only the boys having to sleep on the floor.

The next day the anticipation mounted as we got closer to the Manitoba border, and Father became talkative as the tall evergreens and black soil of his former home appeared.

"They must have had rain lately," he commented. There were huge lakes in some of the grain fields.

"It was a real muddy day when we were married too," Mama reflected. More than ten years ago, she had arrived from South

Hampton, England, where she had been detained a year longer than her family who had settled in Coaldale Alberta. But her fiance, David, who had been able to emigrate earlier, without any trouble, had started farming with his brother Martin in Arnaud where the rest of his family had settled. Their regular correspondence kept the flames of love burning in their hearts over the long months of impatient waiting. Her vivid imagination had conjured up idyllic things they would do together after three years of separation.

Father broke the silence.

"There was a Swedish bachelor living next to us that kept saying, 'Vy you vait for a gurl dat haf sick eyes? Lots of purty gurls here to marry.' Then when your mother finally did come, he came to me at the wedding and said, "Dafid, you shmart to vait for hur." Father smiled.

Mother's eyes had that faraway look. They had married August 25, only days after she came, right in the thick of harvest time. After the interminable wait, her permission to leave and come unexpectedly, and there was no place for her to stay, so the wedding had to happen quickly. The morning after the big celebration in the community hall, her husband had to be up and away with the threshing crew and she had been left to do the chores. Not that she was a stranger to farm work, but she could still remember the waves of disillusionment that had come over her, as she tried to collect the cows for the milking at night. They were grazing in the slough grass amongst the willows by the creek, resisting her efforts to round them up. And the swarms of mosquitoes were determined to eat her alive. Tears of disappointment trickled down her face. She had been teaching herself to play some songs on the piano, so she could surprise David. Whatever had given her the idea that there was a piano in this pioneer place? She had dreamed of fixing his favorite, dishes, with a bouquet of flowers on the table. They didn't even have their own place to live, sharing the upstairs with his brother's family. The relatives were all very kind, but pre-occupied with their own affairs and the urgency and busyness of harvesting the garden produce that would sustain them through the winter.

And the bed bugs! Dear God! Russia had never been like this, or had she forgotten? She had taken the bed frame apart and literally washed it in kerosene, then gone over the mattress inch by inch, and squeezed the creatures between her fingernails. She had stopped counting at a hundred. And David had never known when she cried herself to sleep at night, People had been kind, but she was lonesome for her family, none of whom had been able to come to the wedding from Coaldale. He was too exhausted to even to have the bed-bugs bother him.

Will Grandma and Grandpa be expecting us? Victor asked.

"Oh yes, we'll phone them from Winnipeg!" Father liked to play a trick on them He would call, disguising his voice and ask in Russian, whether they would be willing to take guests for the night and see how long it took for them to catch on to who he was.

It would still take several hours to get to Arnaud. Time to practise the song again, and then continue on, as the memorized verses of other songs came back to them. The ground was so black here, and there were so many evergreens and sloughs and patches of uncleared brush. At long last the new house with its windowed veranda came into view. Uncle John had built it on the old homestead and it had brick tar paper siding and a lightning deflector. The house was ablaze with lights. Shouts of greeting intermingled as portly Grandma and soft, curvy-plump Aunt Mary with her twinkling eyes folded us into their arms. Grandpa's resonant voice loudly exuded his excited welcome, with Uncle John standing by, awaiting his turn to hug us all.

A voice shook me out of my reverie, as I looked at my son beside me.

"What's in that letter, Mom?' he asked.

"We're going to have a reunion!" I answered emotionally, and I hugged him to myself.

www.ingramcontent.com/pod-product-compliance
Lightning Source LLC
LaVergne TN
LVHW010120170826
845678LV00012B/2511

* 9 7 8 1 9 9 0 3 8 9 0 6 1 *